INVESTIGATING

PLANET EARTH

SUPER COOL SCIENCE EXPERIMENTS

CHERRY LAKE PRESS

Ann Arbor, Michigan

SCIENCE INVESTIGATION

by Matt Mullins

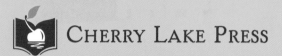

CHERRY LAKE PRESS

Published in the United States of America by
Cherry Lake Publishing Group
Ann Arbor, Michigan
www.cherrylakepublishing.com

Reading Adviser: Beth Walker Gambro, MS, Ed., Reading Consultant, Yorkville, IL

Content Editor: Robert Wolffe, EdD,
Professor of Teacher Education, Bradley University, Peoria, Illinois

Book Designer: Ed Morgan of Bowerbird Books

Grateful acknowledgment to Deborah Simon, Department of Chemistry, Whitman College

Photo Credits: 9, 10, 13,15 top, 17, 18, 21, 22, 25, 26, The Design Lab; 23, Engabreen, Svartisen glacier, Meløy, Nordland, Norway. Photo: Guttorm Raknes (drguttorm) July 2004/Wikimedia Commons.

Copyright © 2024 by Cherry Lake Publishing

All rights reserved. No part of this book may be reproduced or utilized in any form or by any means without written permission from the publisher.

Cherry Lake Press is an imprint of Cherry Lake Publishing Group.

Library of Congress Cataloging-in-Publication Data has been filed and is available at catalog.loc.gov

Printed in the United States of America
Corporate Graphics

A Note to Parents and Teachers: Please review the instructions for these experiments before your children do them. Be sure to help them with any experiments you do not think they can safely conduct on their own.

A Note to Kids: Be sure to ask an adult for help with these experiments when you need it. Always put your safety first!

Note from Publisher: Websites change regularly, and their future contents are outside of our control. Supervise children when conducting any recommended online searches for extended learning opportunities.

CONTENTS

A Special
PLANET

There are many things that make Earth special. One of the most amazing things about our planet is its oceans. Did you know that 70 percent of Earth's surface is covered in water? Our special planet also has an **atmosphere** with lots of oxygen for us to breathe.

Just because Earth is our home doesn't mean we know everything about it. In fact, there's much to learn! Maybe you've wondered about Earth's shape or how the air, land, and oceans change over time. If so, you're thinking like a scientist. In this book, we'll carry out experiments about Earth just like professional scientists. We'll even learn how to design our own experiments!

Getting STARTED

Scientists learn about Earth by studying it. Astronomers study space and Earth's relationship to the solar system. Volcanologists study volcanoes and eruptions. Climatologists study the atmosphere and weather patterns. And there are many more Earth scientists.

To better understand what they're studying, scientists perform experiments. They write down their **observations** and discoveries, which often leads to new questions and experiments.

When scientists design experiments, they often use the scientific method. What is the scientific method? It's a step-by-step process to answer specific questions. The steps don't always follow the same pattern. However, the scientific method often works like this:

STEP ONE: A scientist gathers the facts and makes observations about one particular thing.

STEP TWO: The scientist comes up with a question that is not answered by observations and facts.

STEP THREE: The scientist creates a **hypothesis**. This is a statement about what the scientist thinks might be the answer to the question.

STEP FOUR: The scientist tests the hypothesis by designing an experiment to see whether the hypothesis is correct. Then the scientist carries out the experiment and writes down what happens.

STEP FIVE: The scientist draws a **conclusion** based on the result of the experiment. The conclusion might be that the hypothesis is correct. Sometimes, though, the hypothesis is not correct. In that case, the scientist might develop a new hypothesis and another experiment.

You will use the scientific method as you do the experiments in this book. You'll observe Earth and the Moon, how oceans help keep temperatures stable, and how the air we breathe has weight. You'll develop hypotheses, test them, and draw conclusions. In other words, you'll think like a scientist. Ready? Let's get going!

• EXPERIMENT 1 •

Earth Is a Sphere

For thousands of years, people wondered about Earth's shape. Some thought Earth was flat like a pancake or gently curved like a turtle shell. The fact is Earth is shaped like a giant ball or sphere that's a little pudgier at the **equator**. Some scientists describe the shape as an **ellipsoid**.

More than 2,000 years ago, the Greek philosopher Aristotle observed evidence for a sphere-shaped Earth. He saw an **eclipse** where Earth was positioned between the Sun and the Moon. This caused a curved shadow to fall on the Moon. Aristotle believed that only a sphere could cast curved shadows. Is this true? What do you think? Come up with a hypothesis. Here's one option: **A sphere always casts a round shadow.**

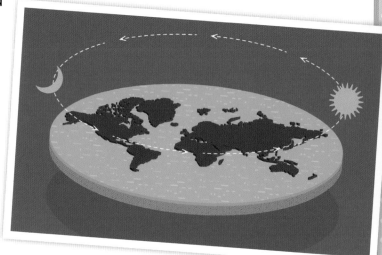

Some ancient people wrongly believed Earth is flat.

Here's what you'll need:

- A room that is dark
- A lamp without its shade
- A table
- A small box
- A clean, empty soup can
- A Frisbee
- A ball

· INSTRUCTIONS ·

1. Find a room that blocks outside light. A room without windows works well as does one with curtains or blinds. Set up a lamp on a table several feet away from a wall. Turn off the lights in the room.

2. Turn on the lamp. Stand between the lamp and the wall. Hold the box and position it so that it casts a shadow on the wall. Focus on the shadow that the box creates. Turn the box in different directions to make new shadows. Can you make a round shadow with the box? Write down what you observe.

3. Now use the soup can to create shadows. Turn it and make as many different shadows as you can. Are the shadows always round? Can you make a rectangular shadow with the can?

4. Test the Frisbee. What kinds of shadows can you make?

5. Test the ball. Turn it in every direction you can think of. Are the shadows always round?

· CONCLUSION ·

Which object made shadows that were always round? Was it the ball? The ball is a sphere. Does this help explain your results? Did any other objects cast round shadows? The Frisbee is round. But it is not a sphere. It is a disk. Did the Frisbee always cast a round shadow? Why or why not? Was your hypothesis correct?

FACTS!

The Sun and the Moon are made of totally different matter. The Sun is a ball of burning gas. The Moon is solid rock. The Moon looks bright because it reflects sunlight like a mirror.

EXPERIMENT 2

The Earth, Sun, and Moon

Earth is the third of eight planets that circle a big star, the Sun, in our solar system. Earth rotates on its **axis** as it **orbits** the Sun. It takes 1 year for Earth to make this trip. And the Moon orbits Earth. It's so big and heavy that, like the Sun, it creates a pull on Earth. We call this force **gravity**. The Sun, Moon, Earth, and other large objects all have a gravitational pull.

The Sun is very bright and hard to look at directly. So how do scientists study it? They use many different tools such as telescopes and satellites. These different tools have helped scientists determine the **diameter** of the Sun and Moon.

Do you think you could make a tool at home for observing the Sun? A pinhole camera is a simple device in which light passes through a tiny hole into a darkened box. Could a pinhole camera help us determine the diameter of the Sun? Here is one hypothesis to test: **A pinhole camera can be used as a tool to measure the Sun's diameter.**

Here's what you'll need:

- A large cardboard box
- A box cutter
- Scissors
- Aluminum foil
- Tape
- A safety pin
- White paper
- A pencil
- A ruler or tape measure
- Notebook paper
- A calculator

· INSTRUCTIONS ·

1. Have an adult help you cut a square into 1 side of the box with the box cutter. The square should be 3/4 by 3/4 inch (1.9 by 1.9 centimeters).

2. Use scissors to cut a square of aluminum foil and tape it over the hole. It should completely cover the hole.

3. Ask an adult to help you push the safety pin through the center of the foil.

4. Tape a piece of white paper inside the box on the side opposite the pinhole.

5. Stand outside in a sunny spot. Turn your back to the Sun. Put the box over your head so that you're looking at the white paper. You may have to take some time to adjust the box so that you don't block the pinhole.

6. Have someone hold the box in place once you find the correct setup. You should see an image of the Sun shining on the white paper. Mark the paper with a pencil along both sides of the image.

7. Take the box off your head. Use the ruler or tape measure to measure the distance between the pinhole and the white paper. Then measure the distance in centimeters between your pencil marks. Write down the numbers on a piece of paper.

8. To determine the diameter of the Sun, you need to know that the distance from Earth to the Sun is 149,600,000 kilometers (92,957,130 miles). Now use a calculator and follow these steps:

(a) Divide the diameter of the image of the Sun by the distance from the pinhole to the sheet of paper.

(b) Take that number and multiply it by the distance from Earth to the Sun.

(c) The number you come up with is the diameter of the Sun in kilometers. Write down your answer.

· CONCLUSION ·

What number did you get for the diameter of the Sun? Was it close to 1,392,000 kilometers (864,949 miles)? Was your pinhole camera a good tool for determining the diameter? Why or why not?

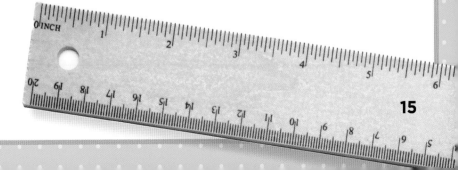

Water and Temperature

Humans and other living things need Earth's oceans to survive. One of the most important things the oceans do is keep the planet's temperatures stable. But how? Think about a desert where there is little water. It gets very hot during the day and is cold at night. Soil and rock absorb heat from the Sun. But how well do they hold on to that heat? Could water have the ability to retain heat better than soil and rock? Could this be a reason behind water's role in regulating the climate? Here's one hypothesis: **Water retains heat better than soil.**

Here's what you'll need:

- 3 identical, clean aluminum cans
- A kitchen scale
- Garden soil
- Sand
- Water
- Plastic wrap
- A thermometer
- A sheet of cardboard
- Black cloth
- A cookie sheet
- An oven
- Oven mitts
- A cutting board

· INSTRUCTIONS ·

1. Place 1 can on the scale and add 7 ounces (198.4 grams) of soil to it. Weigh the second can, and add 7 ounces of sand to it. Repeat the process to add 7 ounces of water to the last can.

2. Cover the can of water with plastic wrap. Let all 3 cans sit overnight. The next day, use your thermometer to check the temperature of each material. Write down the temperatures.

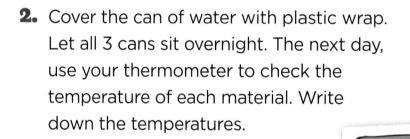

3. Place a sheet of cardboard in a sunny spot. Put the cans on the cardboard. Each can should get the same amount of sunlight. Place the black cloth over the cans. The cloth will help the cans heat up faster.

4. Check the temperature of each material every 20 minutes for 2 hours. Record the temperatures.

5. Place the cans on a cookie sheet. Ask an adult to help you put the cookie sheet in an oven warmed to 120° Fahrenheit (48.9° Celsius). Leave the cans in the oven for 20 minutes. Have your adult helper take the cookie sheet and cans out of the oven. Carefully measure the temperature of each substance.

6. Use an oven mitt to place each can on a cutting board in a cool place.

7. Carefully record the temperature of each material every 20 minutes for 2 hours.

• CONCLUSION •

Review your data. During Step #4, which material heated up the fastest? The slowest? During Step #7, which substance cooled down the fastest? The slowest? Which material would you say heated up the slowest and cooled down the slowest? This material retains heat well and keeps temperatures more even than the other materials. Was it water? Was your hypothesis correct?

19

Glaciers at Work

Earth's surface is constantly changing. For example, volcanoes erupt. Large underground plates of rock shift and cause earthquakes. And frozen rivers of ice known as glaciers slowly move across the land. Scientists know that glaciers covered many parts of the world thousands of years ago. These glaciers carved and changed the land as they passed over it. How? Glaciers tend to pick up rocks as they slide along. Could this have something to do with their ability to carve Earth's surface? And what happens when a glacier melts? Come up with a hypothesis. Here is one option:

A glacier can transform a landscape and deposit materials as it melts.

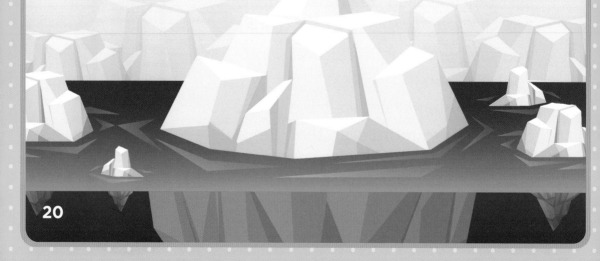

Here's what you'll need:

- A dish towel
- A sunny windowsill
- An ice cube
- Sand
- A flat bar of soap

FACTS!

For decades, scientists have observed that Earth is warming. They use **satellites** and other tools to collect information about the land, atmosphere, ocean, and ice. This information tells us that the warmest years ever recorded happened in the last 20 years! As Earth warms, glaciers and ice sheets melt. Sea levels rise. The water gets warmer, too. These changes can cause flooding and harm ocean animals and plants. The more you learn about climate change, the more you can take action to do something about it!

· INSTRUCTIONS ·

1. Lay the dish towel on a sunny windowsill.

2. Dip one side of the ice cube in the sand so that it's well covered.

3. Place the bar of soap on the towel.

4. Put the ice cube, sandy-side down, on the bar of soap. Press the ice cube down a little and slide it across the soap. How does this change the surface of the soap?

5. Dip the same side of the ice cube in the sand to give it another coating.

6. Place the cube, sandy-side down, on the soap. Let the ice completely melt in the sunlight. Write down what you observe after the ice has melted.

· CONCLUSION ·

The bar of soap represents a landscape. The ice cube is a glacier. The sand represents the stones and Earthy matter that glaciers collect as they move along. How did rubbing the ice affect the soap? Did it become rough or grooved? What does this tell us about how glaciers change the land? What about when the ice cube melted? Did it deposit, or leave behind, the sand?

In nature, glaciers are much heavier than your ice cube. Their weight helps them dig deeply into Earth's surface. In fact, glaciers have helped carve out huge lakes. What would happen if you pushed the ice cube harder into the soap as you scraped? Try it. Was your hypothesis correct? Why or why not?

There are glaciers in many northern parts of the world. This glacier is located in Norway.

· EXPERIMENT 5 ·

The Amazing Atmosphere

Earth's atmosphere is the thick layer of gases that wraps around our planet. Did you know that air has weight? A small amount of air may not weigh a lot. But the weight of a lot of air adds up. For example, the air above a 1-inch (2.5 cm) square space weighs about 15 pounds (6.8 kilograms). And the air above a 2-inch (5.1 cm) square has a whopping 30 pounds (13.6 kg) of **pressure**. That's enough pressure to hold something in place! Could there be a way to visually demonstrate that air has weight? Could air pressure be used to help hold something in place, such as a yardstick? Here are two possible hypotheses:

Hypothesis #1: Atmospheric pressure is strong enough to hold a yardstick in place.

Hypothesis #2: Atmospheric pressure is not strong enough to hold a yardstick in place.

Here's what you'll need:

- A thin, lightweight, wooden yardstick
- A table
- Padded glove
- Safety goggles
- A sheet of newspaper

FACTS!

Earth's atmosphere has six different layers. They stretch from the planet's surface all the way to space. They are the troposphere, stratosphere, mesosphere, thermosphere, ionosphere, and exosphere.

·INSTRUCTIONS·

1. Place the yardstick on the table. Less than half of it should extend beyond the edge of the table.

2. Put on the glove and safety goggles. Give the stick a quick karate chop near the end that's off the table. Be careful not to get hit by the yardstick! What happens to the yardstick? Write down your observations.

3. Reposition the yardstick on the table in the same way as Step #1.

4. Open a full sheet of newspaper and lay it over the yardstick. The crease should run along the length of the yardstick. Lay the paper evenly so it spreads out an equal distance over both sides of the stick. Smooth it down so that it hugs the table and yardstick and there are no air pockets.

5. Karate chop the yardstick in the same spot. What happens? Write down what you observe.

CONCLUSION

Did the yardstick fly up the first time you struck it? How were your results different when the yardstick was covered by the newspaper? By spreading the newspaper out, you created a wider area for atmospheric pressure to weigh down one end of the yardstick. The force of the weight of the air across all of the paper is strong. This extra downward force kept the end of the stick from lifting up as it did the first time you struck it. By chopping quickly, air couldn't slip in under the newspaper and help lift it. All of that atmospheric pressure was bearing down on the paper and on one end of the yardstick! That pressure on the newspaper was greater than the force of your blow to the other end of the stick. Does this explain your results? Was your hypothesis correct?

FACTS!

The air we breathe contains oxygen. But did you know that it contains other gases, too? Air contains about 78 percent nitrogen, 21 percent oxygen, and 1 percent of other gases!

· EXPERIMENT 6 ·

Do It Yourself!

Greenhouse gases form a layer in the atmosphere that traps heat. That's a good thing. These gases let sunlight pass through the atmosphere. But they prevent the heat that the sunlight brings from leaving the atmosphere. Earth's surface would be much cooler without those gases. This is called the **greenhouse effect**.

However, human activity is changing the greenhouse effect. For example, when humans burn coal and oil, they release huge amounts of carbon dioxide into the air. This and other gases can trap more heat, resulting in a greater greenhouse effect and a warmer planet.

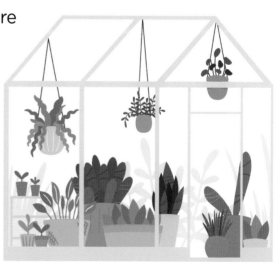

A greenhouse is a building that's usually made from glass. Greenhouses trap heat—much like the atmosphere traps heat!

How could you design an experiment about global warming and the greenhouse effect? You could use two plastic containers with a thermometer in each. Cover one container with a tight layer of plastic wrap to represent a thicker "blanket" of gases. Leave the other uncovered. Do you think one container will get warmer in the sunlight? Come up with a hypothesis and test it. Give it a try, young scientist!

FACTS!

You've learned a lot about Earth. Pick one thing about Earth that interests you the most, such as plant life, the water cycle, ecosystems, weather, or any other topic. Then use your skills as a scientist to investigate and experiment!

Glossary

atmosphere (at-MUHS-fear) the blanket of gases that surrounds Earth

axis (AK-sis) the line about which a rotating body, such as Earth, turns

conclusion (kuhn-KLOO-zhuhn) a final decision, thought, or opinion

diameter (dye-AM-uh-tur) the distance across a circle in a straight line

eclipse (ih-KLIPS) the blocking from view of one object in space by another

ellipsoid (ih-LIP-soid) a shape like a sphere that may be longer in one or more directions like an egg

equator (ih-KWAY-tur) the imaginary line halfway between the North and South Poles that runs around the middle of Earth

gravity (GRAV-uh-tee) the force by which all objects in the universe are attracted to each other

greenhouse effect (GREEN-houss uh-FEKT) the warming of Earth's surface caused by gases that collect in the atmosphere and prevent the Sun's heat from escaping

hypothesis (hy-POTH-uh-sihss) a logical guess about what will happen in an experiment

observations (ob-zur-VAY-shuhnz) things that are seen or noticed with one's senses

orbits (OR-bitss) travels around a sun or a planet

pressure (PRESH-ur) the force produced by pressing on something

satellites (SAT-uh-lites) spacecrafts that send information back to Earth

For More Information

BOOKS

Baumann, Anne-Sophie. *The Ultimate Book of Planet Earth*. San Francisco: Chronicle Books, 2019.

Feldstein, Stephanie. *Save Ocean Life*. Ann Arbor: Cherry Lake Press, 2023.

Kurtz, Kevin. *Climate Change and Rising Temperatures*. Minneapolis: Lerner Publishing, 2019.

Planet Earth. New York: DK Publishing, 2022.

WEBSITES
Explore these online sources with an adult:

Britannica Kids: Earth

Nasa Space Place: All About Earth

PBS Kids: Ready Jet Go! Mission Earth

Index

About the Author

Matt Mullins holds a master's degree in the history of science. He lives in Madison, Wisconsin, but he hasn't always. When he was 14, he awoke one morning and saw everything outside covered in fine, gray ash. It was May 18, 1980. Mount Saint Helens, which was not even 35 miles (56.3 km) away, had just erupted.